Me and My Pet
RABBIT

Christine Morley and Carole Orbell

Illustrations by
Brita Granström

World Book

in association with

WⒸC4N

Published in the United States and Canada by
World Book Inc.
525 W. Monroe
Chicago, IL 60661
in association with Two-Can Publishing Ltd.

**For information on other World Book products,
call 1-800-255-1750, x 2238 or visit us at our Web site
at http://www.worldbook.com**

Art director: Carole Orbell
Senior Managing Editor: Christine Morley
Designer: Lisa Nutt
Consultant: Lisa Cobb, United Kingdom's Animal Nurse of the Year 1995
Illustrator: Brita Granström
Photographer: John Englefield
U.S. editors: Karen Ingebretsen and Melissa Tucker,
  World Book Publishing

Morley, Christine.
   Me and my pet rabbit / Christine Morley and Carole Orbell;
illustrations by Brita Granström.
      p.   cm.
   Summary: A practical discussion of how to keep rabbits safely at
home, what kind of environment to provide for them, what to feed
them, and how to breed them.
   ISBN 0-7166-1797-8 (hardcover). -- ISBN 0-7166-1798-6 (softcover)
   1. Rabbits as pets--Juvenile literature. [1. Rabbits as pets.
2. Pets.] I. Orbell, Carole. II. Granström, Brita, ill.
III. Title.
SF453.2.M67 1997
636.9'322--DC21   96-50420

Printed in Hong Kong

2 3 4 5 6 7 8 9 10 02 01 00 99 98 (soft cover)
2 3 4 5 6 7 8 9 10 02 01 00 99 98 (hard cover)

Contents

Furry friends

Everyone loves rabbits. They are cuddly, playful, and easy to take care of. But if you want to keep rabbits, you need to know how to care for these cute creatures properly.

Different rabbits

Rabbits have been around for thousands of years. Some live in the wild, while others live as pets in people's homes. Wild rabbits are small and brown, but pet rabbits can be many colors.

The first one to jump gets the lettuce.

Rabbits are lovable animals and they really enjoy being petted.

Your own sweetheart

Many years ago, children called their pet rabbits "sweethearts" because they loved them so much. Show your rabbit you love it by petting and talking to it.

Victorian children loved to keep pet rabbits.

Country cousins

Wild rabbits live in the country in homes dug in the ground. These are called warrens and are made up of lots of rooms joined together by tunnels. Rabbits stay in the warren during the day and then come out to nibble on grass and plants in the early morning and evening, when it is quiet.

Mmm, that grass looks very tasty.

Girl rabbits burrow to make warrens.

Wild ways

Although pet rabbits are much friendlier than wild ones, they still do lots of things that wild rabbits do. They like to hop around nibbling grass, and they use their big ears and twitching noses to sense what's around them.

All shapes and sizes

There are lots of types, or breeds, of rabbits around today. In fact, there are over 100. You can choose from cute little Dwarf rabbits to bunnies with thick, fluffy fur or large, floppy ears.

Some rabbits are too big for small hands to pick up.

Colorful coats

Pet rabbits come in a variety of beautiful colors, from golden-brown to black. Some are the same color all over, while others have patches, spots, and even stripes on their coats.

Little and large

Rabbits can be all sizes. The White Flemish Giant breed is bigger than some dogs! Netherland Dwarf rabbits, however, are very small and weigh as little as a bag of sugar.

Dwarf rabbits like us don't take up much room!

Soft and smooth

All rabbits have soft fur to keep them warm. Some, such as Rex breeds, have short coats that feel like velvet. Angora rabbits have long, fluffy fur, often called wool. People use the wool to knit sweaters.

Show time

Rabbit clubs often put on shows where you can see many breeds of rabbits. To find a club, write to: American Rabbit Breeders Association, Inc., PO Box 426, Bloomington, IL 61702.

Big ears are best!

Most rabbits have long, upright ears. Some rabbits, called Lops, have floppy ears. Lops cannot hear as well as rabbits with upright ears.

Visit a rabbit show to see some beautiful bunnies.

The right rabbit

Before buying a rabbit, think about how much care, attention, and space it will need. You will have to look after your rabbit all its life – which may be up to five years!

There's no way I'll fit in there.

Which breed?
It's important to think about what size of rabbit you want. Small- and medium-sized rabbits need less space than large rabbits, and they're easier to pick up too. If you want a young rabbit, make sure you know how big it will grow.

Long or short?
Long-haired rabbits look lovely, but they need more grooming than short-haired ones. Angora rabbits have coats that grow to a length of 4¾ inches (12 centimeters), so they need to be brushed every day.

One or more?
Rabbits can get lonely, so keep more than one if you can. Girl rabbits get along well, but boy rabbits will fight, unless they have grown up together and have plenty of space. Don't keep a boy and girl rabbit in the same cage, unless you want them to breed, or have babies.

Boy rabbits may fight if they live together.

Lonesome bunny

If you can't keep two rabbits, why not buy a guinea pig to keep your rabbit company? Guinea pigs and rabbits get along very well, but they need to be fed separately and put in their own hutches at night.

We may not be looking the same way...

...but we're best friends, really!

Sisters will get along well with each other.

Are you ready?

Before you bring your bunny home, make sure you have a comfortable home ready. It will need a roomy hutch, tasty food, plenty of water, and lots of hugs!

No place like home

Rabbits are usually kept outside in a house called a hutch. You can buy one from a pet store, or ask an adult to make one. It must be big enough for your rabbit to move around in and to stand up in. In winter, the hutch should be moved indoors.

This is the best-kept hutch in town.

Make sure your rabbit has lots of clean straw and fresh food.

1 water bottle
2 newspapers
3 straw
4 hay rack

A happy hutch

Rabbits should be sheltered from the wind, the rain, and the hot sun.

I'm as snug as a bug in a rug.

Blankets will keep a bunny dry in wet weather.

Food and water

Inside the hutch, you will need a hay rack and a water bottle to keep your rabbit's food and water clean. The bottom of the hutch should be lined with newspaper and covered by wood shavings or cat litter. Finally, add plenty of fresh straw to keep your bunny snug.

Rabbits like to hear friendly chatter, so keep the hutch very close to your home.

The great indoors

You can also keep your rabbit inside your house. You will need a special cage for it to sleep in, and you will have to make sure it has a safe area to run around in. Turn to page 20 to find out more.

Choosing your pal

Most rabbits are cuddly and cute, and you'll probably want every one you see. But before you buy, here are a few tips on how to find and choose a healthy rabbit.

The best bunny
A healthy rabbit should have a clean, shiny coat and bright eyes. Its ears and under its tail should be clean, and its claws should not be too long.

When you buy a rabbit
When you have found a rabbit you like, find out if it's a boy or girl. And, if you want other rabbits, ask if there are any from the same family for sale.

Take your time choosing your rabbit from a good pet store.

Hop to the store

A pet store is the usual place to buy a rabbit. But if you want a special breed, you may need to go to a breeder. You can find one through rabbit clubs or rabbit magazines.

Home and dry

Take your rabbit home in a strong carrying box. Make sure the box has air holes in it so your rabbit can breathe. Try not to jostle the rabbit, and keep your journey as short as possible.

Let your new rabbit settle in before your friends crowd around.

Settling in

When you bring your rabbit home, it may feel scared. Make sure its hutch is comfortable and give it fresh food and water. Let it explore its new home, but come back often to check that it's settling in.

Feeling hungry

Pet rabbits spend most of their days nibbling, just like wild ones! Give your bunny plenty of fresh food and clean water every day to keep it happy and full of energy.

Never feed a rabbit plants with pesticides on them.

1 pear
2 turnip
3 celery
4 cucumber
5 mushrooms
6 peas
7 tomato

Food for free
Dandelions, chickweed, and clover can be found in the garden and are good for rabbits. But always ask an adult if you have pulled up the right plants, because some, such as bindweed, are poisonous.

Magic mix
Every morning, give your rabbit fresh fruit and vegetables with about half a cup of pellets or cereals. This mix of food should give your rabbit all the nutrients it needs. Some hay at night helps your rabbit's digestion.

Crisp and crunchy

Lettuce, broccoli, and other types of greens make a good evening snack for your rabbit. But don't give it too much lettuce, which can cause diarrhea.

More or less?

If your bunny gobbles up everything quickly, you could give it a little more. If your pet always leaves food uneaten, cut down on how much you give it. Always take away food that is left, or it will rot.

Keep bunnies away from vegetable patches!

What a feast! Is it my birthday?

Neat and tidy

Rabbits keep their coats clean and shiny all by themselves. But if you give them a gentle brushing regularly, it will get them used to being handled. They really enjoy it, too!

Keeping clean

Watch your rabbit to see how it cleans itself. It uses its front teeth to pick out bits of dirt and then licks its coat with its tongue. This covers the fur with oil, which protects it. To clean its face, first it licks its paws, then it wipes them over its ears.

Rabbits like to wash themselves several times a day.

Now where did I put that mirror?

Hair care

Short-haired rabbits can be brushed once a week. Gently brush the fur toward the tail – don't forget the tummy. Long-haired rabbits need to be brushed every day to keep their fur from getting tangled.

Your hair could do with a brushing, too!

Up and away

To groom your rabbit properly, you need to know how to pick it up safely. Put one hand in front of it, then slide the other hand under its back legs. Hold it close along your arm or with its head over your shoulder. Never lift your rabbit up by its ears or legs.

Is this what's called a bunny hug?

Winter coat

In the winter, your rabbit grows a thick coat to keep it warm. As the weather turns warmer, it loses this coat. This is called molting. Regular brushing helps to remove loose hairs when your rabbit is molting.

Never bathe your bunny—this will wash out the special oil in its coat.

Getting down

To put your rabbit down, turn it around so it faces away from you and put down the back feet first. This way, your bunny cannot kick out and scratch you if it gets frightened.

Keeping fit

Playing with your rabbit is great fun and helps keep it fit, too. Let your bunny play outside as much as possible, but keep it in a run, so that you can catch it again!

Run, rabbit, run!

If you build a run next to your rabbit's hutch, it can hop around whenever it feels like it. Make sure the fence goes into the ground, or that the bottom of the run is covered with wire mesh, so your rabbit can't dig under it.

Garden games

You can let your rabbit play in a yard, as long as there is a strong fence around it. Watch out for cats or dogs that might scare your rabbit.

A good game to play is to bury food for your bunny to sniff out and dig up.

So this is what it's like in a submarine.

A long piece of pipe is safe and fun for rabbits to explore.

I don't need ice cream to stay cool.

Moving around

Ask an adult to make a triangular-shaped run that can be moved around the yard. This way your rabbit can nibble fresh grass every day. Remember to leave a bowl of water in the run and keep it shaded from the sun.

A colorful painted plant pot makes a great toy for a rabbit.

Hard to catch

Your rabbit will enjoy being outdoors in a run and sometimes won't want to go back into the hutch! You will have to be very patient and shoo it into a corner. Never run after it or grab it – your rabbit will only get more scared and difficult to catch.

Indoor bunny

If you don't have a yard, your rabbit will be quite happy living indoors. Just make sure it spends most of the day out of its cage, hopping around the house.

Always watch your bunny – it could get into dangerous spots!

Hutch-free zone
You won't need a hutch for your indoor bunny. Instead, a large, wire cage will do as its bedroom at night. During the day, your rabbit should run free or have a large playpen to explore.

Playing safe
Make your home safe by hiding sharp objects, such as scissors, and moving electrical wires, which your rabbit might chew. Close all doors so it can't wander into unsafe places.

Rabbits love company and like being part of the family.

Keep dogs on leashes or they might frighten your rabbit.

Bad bunny

Sometimes your rabbit will misbehave, by chewing your favorite toy, or going to the bathroom on the carpet. If you catch it misbehaving, say "No" firmly, and squirt it with water from a spray bottle. Never shout at or hit your rabbit.

Ooops! I'm not supposed to kick the sawdust.

Toilet training

A rabbit can be trained to use a litter box as a toilet. Line the box with newspaper and cover it with wood shavings or cat litter. If you put your rabbit in the box after it eats, it'll soon learn to use the box.

With a little training, your bunny can use a litter box.

Routine care

Your rabbit likes its home to be cleaned every day. Keep the hutch nice and fresh by taking away uneaten food and dirty bedding.

Cleaning kit

1 bottle brushes
2 dustpan and brush
3 scrubbing brush
4 rubber gloves
5 bucket
6 soap
7 scraper

You will need all the items shown here when cleaning out the hutch. Remember to wear rubber gloves when picking up dirty bedding. And use only disinfectant that's made for animals – you can buy this from pet stores.

Now that's clean.

Dirt busters!

Replace dirty or wet bedding daily with clean, dry wood shavings and straw. Once a week, sweep the hutch, then rinse it with hot, soapy water and spray it with animal disinfectant. Always make sure the hutch is completely dry before putting your rabbit back in.

Rabbit droppings and dirty straw can be put on a compost heap.

Bottles and bowls

Every day, empty and wash the food bowl and water bottle. Once a week, you should scrub the bottle, lid, and tube well. You can buy special long brushes for this job.

When you go on vacation, leave your rabbit in safe hands.

Bon voyage!

When you go on vacation, find a friend or neighbor to care for your bunny. Before you go, clean out the hutch and make sure there is plenty of food and bedding. Write down a list of things that the caregiver must do, as well as what food your bunny likes and dislikes. Remember to leave your vet's telephone number and address.

Bunny talk

The noises and movements your rabbit makes are its way of talking to you. As you get to know your rabbit, you'll be able to tell when it's hungry, when it wants to play, and when it wants to rest.

When your bunny licks your finger it means it really likes you.

On the scent
To be friendly your rabbit will rub its head against you or will lick your hands and fingers with its tongue. This leaves a special scent on you that only rabbits and other animals can smell.

All sorts of smells
Your rabbit's nose will twitch a lot when other rabbits are around. This is because it recognizes them by their smell. Sometimes it will rub its scent on other rabbits. This way, it knows that they're friends.

Now you smell just like me!

Danger signals

Wild rabbits have to keep watch for dangerous animals. Pet rabbits do this, too. If they see or hear something strange, they rise up on their back legs to get a better view. If they sense danger, they thump their back legs. This is a signal for other rabbits to run to safety.

Rabbits are shy and sometimes they will hide from people.

Wild rabbits wag their tails as a warning.

Angry bunnies

When rabbits are angry, they will stare at each other and scratch the ground with their front paws. They will also stamp their back feet and may even try to bite each other!

Watch the TV, not me!

Checkup

Pet rabbits usually stay in good condition, as long as they are properly cared for. Help to keep your rabbit healthy by carrying out the checks on this page.

Use an old kitchen scale to weigh your rabbit.

I must cut down on those carrots!

Weekly weigh-in
It's a good idea to weigh your rabbit every week and write down its weight. If it has become much heavier or lighter, it may be ill. If it puts on weight every week, it might not be getting enough exercise.

Visiting the vet

When you first buy your bunny, take it to the vet for a checkup. The vet will give your rabbit injections to prevent some illnesses, such as myxomatosis. The vet can also perform an operation on your rabbit to stop her (or him) from breeding. This is called neutering.

Clipping claws

If your rabbit's claws grow too long, your vet will trim them. She may even trim your rabbit's teeth, too!

Your vet will look at your bunny's teeth to see if they are too long.

Check your rabbit's claws every month in case they're overgrown.

I wonder if that tickles?

Droppings for dinner!

Don't worry if you see your rabbit eating its own droppings. It may sound very strange to us, but it is quite normal for rabbits! They do it because these droppings still have lots of nutrients left in them.

Feeling sick

Just like people, rabbits get sick from time to time. Unlike people, they can't tell you when they're feeling bad. So here are a few warning signs to watch out for.

Sick or not?

When your rabbit is sick, it will probably stop eating and running around, although it may drink a lot. You should telephone the vet and she will tell you whether she needs to see your rabbit.

Aahhchoo!

Rabbits can catch a disease that is similar to a cold. It is called snuffles. A rabbit with snuffles has a runny nose and sometimes runny eyes. If your rabbit has these symptoms, call the vet quickly.

These fleas are making me hopping mad.

Hop off!

If your bunny starts scratching a lot, look closely in its fur and see if you can spot any tiny, dark specks. These are fleas. Ask an adult to powder your rabbit with flea powder, and spray the hutch with flea spray, too.

Making a note

When you visit your vet, she'll want to know some things about your rabbit's health, such as its age and weight, and what illnesses or injections it has had. Keep this information in a notebook, so that you won't forget anything.

MY RABBIT
Patch

AGE:
6 months

COLOR:
golden brown with a black patch

Take a photo of your bunny to put in your notebook.

Bunnies galore

Everyone loves baby rabbits, but if you decide to breed your rabbit, make sure that you can find good homes for all of the babies.

Does and bucks

To breed rabbits put a doe (girl rabbit) and a buck (boy rabbit) into a hutch for five or six days. After this time, put the doe back in its own cage because it might fight with the buck.

Making a nest

It will be about one month before the doe gives birth. At this time, make the hutch warm and comfortable with soft straw. The doe will pull out some of its own fur to make the nest extra snug.

Babies drink their mother's milk for the first six weeks.

A mother rabbit will need extra food.

Kitten care
After two days, take a peek at the kittens to see if they're moving – that means they are healthy. But don't pick them up until they're three weeks old, as you may upset the mother.

A new family
Your rabbit will probably have its babies at night or early in the morning when it is quiet. You will be excited to see the babies, which are called kittens, but you must not touch the nest for a few days. If you do, the doe may become frightened and attack the kittens.

Even babies like me know how to keep clean.

Friendly owners
The kittens will be ready to leave their mother when they are about seven weeks old. By this time, they will be eating the same food as a grown-up rabbit. You must try to find good homes for all of them. Why not ask your friends if they would like a baby rabbit to keep?

Useful words

agouti A type of wild rabbit with brown, speckled fur. Other rabbits with the same type of speckled fur are said to have agouti fur.

booster These are injections that your rabbit needs to have every year to protect it against diseases.

breed A special type of rabbit, such as a Dutch or an Angora.

breeding When a boy and girl rabbit mate, so they can have baby rabbits.

buck A male rabbit.

crossbreed A rabbit whose parents or grandparents are different breeds, or a mixture of breeds.

doe A female rabbit.

kitten A baby or young rabbit.

litter A group of baby rabbits from the same family.

neutering An operation both male and female rabbits can have to keep them from breeding, or having babies.

pedigree or purebreed Rabbits whose parents, grandparents, and great-grandparents are all the same breed. They will have a special certificate to prove this.

pregnancy The time when the mother carries her babies inside her. This is usually between 28 and 31 days for a rabbit.

vaccinations These are injections that rabbits have to keep them from catching diseases from other animals.

warren The underground tunnels and burrows where wild rabbits live.